Marvelous Margaux

Written by Elizabeth Subrin
Illustrated by Bilal Tahir

Fishtail Publishing

To my parents,
For their endless love and support.

And to my Justun,
For changing my life in all the best ways.

Thank you,
Elizabeth

Illustrations by Bilal Tahir
Back Cover Photo by Pathways Photography
Book design by Fishtail Publishing LLC

Published in the USA by Fishtail Publishing LLC
Indianapolis, IN
www.fishtailpublishing.org

Paperback: 978-1-7333380-7-3
Library of Congress Control Number: 2021900384

www.marvelousmargaux.com

Marvelous Margaux

Written by Elizabeth Subrin
Illustrated by Bilal Tahir

Hi! My name is Margaux.

I'm a kid, just like you,
except I have something
called Dupl5Q.

This condition is unique and can make it hard for me to speak.

I sometimes make weird noises, but only to say that "I enjoy this!"

I like to flap my arms, but please know that I mean no harm.

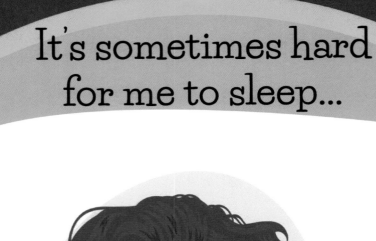

It's sometimes hard
for me to sleep...

Especially if I look too
much at a screen.

I like to jump around...

and even hang
upside down!

I like to play in the water...

and listen to my daddy play his guitar.

I like to dance
and sing to
musical tunes...

and watch
movies
with
cartoons.

I like to look at books...

and eat
anything
that my
mommy
cooks.

I may be a little different,
but please know I'd love to
be your friend.

I have a special friend named Jelly, and she wrote this book to show how much she loves me.

Dup15q Alliance

FOR 15Q 11.2–13.1 MULTIPLICATIONS

Dup15q Syndrome is a rare genetic disorder caused by an extra piece of genetic material on the 15th Chromosome. It is estimated that 1 out of every 5,000 to 8,000 live births will have Dup15q Syndrome.

Genetic testing due to seizures/infantile spasms and/or developmental concerns (developmental delay, intellectual disability, or autism spectrum disorder) is encouraged to get a proper diagnosis.

To learn more visit www.dup15q.org

Made in the USA
Columbia, SC
04 March 2021